The Vineyard

Exploding Grapes

Damon E. Johnson

Creative Talents Unleashed

GENERAL INFORMATION

The Vineyard
Exploding Grapes
By
Damon E. Johnson

1st Edition: 2015

www.ctupublishinggroup.com

Publisher Information
1st Edition: Creative Talents Unleashed
CreativeTalentsUnleashed@aol.com

Copyright © 2015: Damon E. Johnson
Cover Design by Romano Art

ISBN-13: 978-0-9961476-4-4 [Creative Talents Unleashed]
ISBN-10: 0996147640

$13.95

Dedication

To all those who dare to love

Preface

"Like a vintage wine love seeps through our skin quenching hunger's thirst." Dark, rich and full bodied, only begin to describe this wonderful blend of poetry contained in The Vineyard: Exploding Grapes. It is a bouquet of love and desire with a spicy undertone of lust. A very generous wine of words, this second collection of poetry from Damon Johnson takes the reader on a poetic journey, and with its smooth attack it is indeed, full on the palate with a lingering finish.

Table of Contents

Table of Contents . . . continued

Merlot

Table of Contents . . . continued

Table of Contents . . . continued

Riesling

Table of Contents . . . continued

Table of Contents . . . continued

The Vineyard

Exploding Grapes

Damon E. Johnson

Creative Talents Unleashed

Chardonnay

Damon E. Johnson

Exploding Grapes

Like a vintage wine
love seeps through our skin
quenching hunger's thirst
Our bodies intertwine
as heavenly sin
causes passion to
distend and burst

Simple Math

One plus 1
equals 2
But last night
as you laid
your head upon
my chest
the 2 of us
became One

Lie to Me

Tell me I'm not crazy
that our relationship is strong
tell me you still find comfort
in my arms where you belong

Tell me the passion has not died
that I'm the one that you desire
tell me that every time we kiss
I still set your soul on fire

Tell me you'll never leave me
that rumors of our demise are not true
go ahead and just lie to me baby
it's the least that you can do

Some Kind of Wonderful

The dawn wakes up to your smile
the stars envy your light
butterflies think you are beautiful
and eagles marvel at your flight

The trees relax under your shade
the wind sways every time you blow
the river drinks from your mouth
and flowers enjoy watching you grow

Mockingbirds groove to your song
the rainbows admire your hue
even laughter thinks you are funny
and the sunset takes pictures of you

Damon E. Johnson

Hungering

She was once my midnight lover
and the sunlight chased her away
I spent the whole day trying to recover
while my thoughts were in disarray

Her departure left me concerned
and my cravings were hard to fight
I waited anxiously for her return
when she reappeared the very next night

Now that lonely period is far behind
as our excitement grows wild like weeds
can't get her loving off my mind
desire outweighing my emotional needs

My Needs

I need you
to walk with me
to talk with me
to hold me
to console me
to stay with me
to lay with me
to love me
to arch your back
above me
I need you
to address my needs

Wicked

My ex-lover
had some wicked ways
She was a beast in bed
for sure
Our sexual encounters
would last for days
But her attitude
I couldn't endure

Lyrically Speaking

My words are life
unfolding into a song
My words are music
playing soft and long

My words are love
locking you up in forever
My words are laughter
for no reason whatsoever

My words are passion
connecting with your soul
My words are tears
that fall without control

My words are sexy
arousing your desire
My words are fierce
intense like a raging fire

My words are rhythm
keeping you right on time
My words are poetry
stimulating you with my rhyme

Your Cries

I can feel the tremor
inside of your body
as my hands trace the curves
of your womanly figure
while kissing you so deep
my lips swallow your cries

In Your Skin

You have such a warm spirit
that sometimes I want to
climb inside your skin
and channel through
to the rhythm that shakes
your soul to the very bones
Just so I may pretend
for a few moments
that I too
am beautiful

Cloud 9

You are my sunshine
you are my star
I can't help but adore you
just the way you are

You are my rainbow
you are my sky
my life is so incredible
and you're the reason why

You are my lover
you are my best friend
sometimes I really do feel
like I'm walking on the wind

Hurricane

Like a fierce wind
she swept to my bedside
blowing me awake and
sending my body into
an emotional tailspin
I tried to break free
but it was just no use
Her love had me twisted
and I couldn't shake loose

Moist

Words like a river
flow from my mouth
into your patient ears
sending subliminal thoughts
of desire through your mind
as your hands drift south and
rest between your thighs, wet
before you even begin
thinking of me

Following Our Hearts

Our feelings
are deeply rooted
like a tree in its prime
and grow even stronger
as passion calls out to us
in the dark. So when
the sunlight erases
all traces of the night
and splashes in our faces
like fresh water, we are
reminded of what could be
if we truly let love have its way.

Damon E. Johnson

Warm Like Coffee

The sheets on our bed
are crisp and clean
as we lie comfortably
in between

Passion seeps through
our willing skin
and the night seems
to never end

In the morning
our souls will sing
indeed love can be
a refreshing thing

Warm like coffee
holding you
your heart and mine
my favorite brew

Sobering Sunrise

Desire born
of yesterday's promise
now saturates
the sheets of our bed
with hope

Damon E. Johnson

Keeping Strange Hours

Early in the morning
she would often come to me
just to lie skin to skin
We would go a couple of rounds
sometimes as many as three
Enough to last until she comes again

The Love We Make

The love we make
and the time we take
providing comfort whenever
and wherever it's needed,
is proof that our love is real
and that the joy we feel
started from the moment
both of our hearts conceded

Joy Ride

Loving you
is like riding a bicycle
Once you know how
you never forget

You Are My Poem

I don't need a number two pencil
blank sheet of paper or fountain pen
no maple wood desk with a high back chair
or cozy nightlight in the den

No cup of coffee, hot tea or glass of wine
or any exotic kinds of food
the thought of you is motivation enough
to get me in the mood

I don't need total seclusion
just any comfortable place I can find
so I can relax and daydream of you
and write you in my mind

Sonia Sanchez

Your words warm my flesh
shout out to my bones
and whispers love
into my consciousness
as I come alive at the command
of your speaking, seeking tongue

Clean Rinse

Still bitter
from my last love
I now find myself
drinking
from your well
hoping
to wash away
the taste

Damon E. Johnson

Red-Hot Passion

While touching each other
we became so heated
that passion erupted and
sent us rocketing into the air
Then we slowly fell from the sky
and became the sunset

View from the Sidelines
(The Game of Love)

Midway through the 3rd quarter I
can't help but notice that your love
has definitely taken a severe beating.
You've been kicked, tripped, stepped on,
blindsided and illegally tackled out of bounds.
You started off strong, but now you seem
to have grown mentally and physically tired.
Indeed no one can ever question your dedication,
loyalty or total commitment to winning.
And though I must say that I admire your resiliency,
I believe that happiness shouldn't be this difficult.
The truth be told, I've been praying all my life
for an opportunity such as this, and I think
that it's about time that I entered the game.

I'm ready
I'm willing
I'm able
I'm waiting...
Listening for my name.

Damon E. Johnson

I Was Searching

I was searching for understanding
someone to share my joy and tears
I was searching for inspiration
someone to restore my youthful years

I was searching for true love
a faithful companion and loyal friend
the day that I found you
my search came to an end

Merlot

Craving

I want to love somebody
Wrap my arms around their dreams
and arouse their passions
Relate to their everyday struggles
and speak new life into their divine purpose
Find pleasure in their accomplishments
and strength in their occasional tears
Embrace their imperfections
and help cultivate their growth
Listen to their heart and challenge
their opinions when necessary
Be quick to forgive and willing to offer praise
Comfort them during the summer storms
and dance with them throughout
the many blessings of winter
Convey love, even during those times
when words seem inadequate
Give all of myself or give nothing at all
I want to really love somebody
Beginning with me

Medicine Man

Like a once vibrant canary
that has lost the ability to sing
she quietly prayed for change
and waited patiently until
one day he walked into her dreams
carrying a black duffle bag
that contained the antidote
for her long suffering
He opened his bag and removed
a syringe filled with promise
Then climbed down her throat
and injected life into her soul.
And soon her new song became their anthem

Woman

Delicate, warm and sugary sweet
faithful, supportive and strong
compliments seem to fall at her feet
she is as lovely as a robins' song

Her smile is as pleasant as the setting sun
and she has such a sensuous appeal
her sassy attitude is second to none
sometimes she doesn't even appear to be real

The most precious thing earth has ever known
a true angel from the skies above
blessed is the man that finds one of his own
because all she really needs is love

Changing Lanes

Since you been gone
I've been seeing a new kinda lover
Says she likes the way I smell …in the morning

She has to be a gift from heaven,
because she releases such angelic screams
every time I open her up

And when she calls my name
I can't seem to remember the sound
of your voice

Damon E. Johnson

Spiritual Thang

Whenever our tongues
are speaking
while we rub our bodies
together and make
flames

June Jordan

With a stroke of your pen
you feed my hungry spirit
and nurture my growth; like a child
going from a mother's breast to spoon.
Indeed one has never truly experienced love
until they have been caressed by the words of June.

Reflection of Peace

Sometimes, as I hold you next to me
it becomes so peaceful that I can hear my own heartbeat
The rhythm seems to move through my body
alerting me that there is an angel in my presence
Warm, yet so undeniably cool and comforting
Hair so soft and smells like a thousand violets in bloom
Skin so smooth it's like butter flowing through your fingers
Eyes so shiny, they're like two brand new pennies
fresh out of your grandfather's pocket
Lips so full, they're like two slices of an orange so juicy
you can barely wait even one minute to taste them
Body so enticing that you can't help wanting to feel
the cozy wet waves of the ocean that lies inside
leaving the problems of this world behind
swimming blissfully in the solution of love
A journey I would gladly take again and again
but right now, I just want to hold you next to me

Loving Beyond the Flesh

Lying naked in each other's arms
I can feel the essence of your soul
my tongue massages your sweet spot
making you lose control

Slowly I begin to climb on top
careful not to start too deep
you can't help but moan in my ear
uttering secrets meant for you to keep

Now this is how I imagine our connection
coming to a bedroom near you
but only after our conversation reaches perfection
and we can share a common point of view

Don't get me wrong woman I want you
with every fiber of my being
believe that and another thing too
with you, sex is not all that I'm seeing

Damon E. Johnson

Here I Come

I'll be there
to rescue you
before your tears begin
And wrap you up in pleasure
with arms that have no end

Only You

When I kissed your lips
for the very first time
it felt like Christmas day
and the greatest gift was mine

Your love is something special
and truly one of a kind
whenever you leave my arms
I get the urge to press rewind

Damon E. Johnson

Bitter Honey

Just as a bumblebee flutters
among the tall grass,
I ride the wind ever so gently
straight to your window sill
hoping to catch a glimpse of you
in all your sweetness
dancing in the sunrise

But a blue bird mentioned
that you haven't appeared
in quite a few days and
so I must conclude that
you are probably in bed
curled up with a good book
still recovering from my sting

Deep Blue

I discovered that I've grown tired
from yearning for your touch
and my thoughts are uninspired
from missing you too much

My heart just keeps on calling
crying out for you
to rescue me from falling
deeper into blue

Damon E. Johnson

One of These Days

One of these days
you are going to
misuse my love
abuse my love
reject my love
neglect my love
and discover my love
gone

Reality Check

Lately love has lost its luster
and we've ignored it for far too long
simple pleasantries seem difficult to muster
and our chemistry is totally wrong

We don't even express ourselves anymore
silence has replaced our words
love is what we were created for
yet romance has gone to the birds

Don't know when or where we got off track
but we can't continue down this path
it would be good to somehow get our groove back
in fact, it would be nice just to share a laugh

Grey Matters

Dark rain clouds are pouring
while the stream waters are rippling
your unfaithfulness I keep ignoring
cause the thought of losing you is crippling

But the wind of change has indeed spoken
arousing my unconcerned ears
though my spirits are not easily broken
my indifference has now succumbed to tears

Red Wine & Violins

Her heart was committed to another
yet our attraction was obvious to us both
as we quite often pretended not to notice
for fear of being unable to control the desire
that saturated our thirsty bodies without warning.
Denial became useless every time our eyes would meet
and words would quickly disappear behind our smiles.
We were trapped in a situation that appeared to have
only one happy ending. Until she decided to be
a woman content with her promise. While I was
forced to be a man who would have to learn to
respect and live with her choice.

Uncommon

So much more than
a pretty face
Such fiery passion
inside
The true result of
what takes place
When both beauty
and strength
collide

On the Mend

I'm ok
I'm a big boy now
and I sleep all by myself

I'm no longer disenchanted by not having you to hold
And I'm actually kind of getting use to the quiet nights
alone with just my books and a bottle of wine to keep me
company.

I finally got around to changing the sheets and pillow cases
that for weeks seemed to embrace the familiar scent of your
skin. And just yesterday I discarded our favorite comforter.

I even removed your picture from the nightstand.
You know, the one with you wearing that sexy red sundress
I bought while we were in Panama last year.

So you see
I'm ok
I'm a big boy now
and I sleep all by myself.
But sometimes…I cry.

Damon E. Johnson

Yesterday

Your love is now a memory
just like footprints in the sand
washed away by the tide
And as I walk the beach of life
in search of a new love
I find myself constantly
turning around and looking
Hoping to see the past
catching up to me

Strangers in the Night

Two souls
passing through love
on the way to paradise
Freely you come and
reluctantly, I go

Ecstasy

It seems like you're walking on heaven
whenever you stroll my way
your sweet smile erases my worries
and brightens up my day

Sometimes as you hold me close
my heartbeat can be heard
with the softest touch I get butterflies
and you never have to say one word

Below the Surface

Butterflies
butterflies
everywhere
I can feel them
beneath your navel
when I touch you there

Lovecycle

Waking up next to you
is the best part of my day.

At work, I often find myself
putting off tasks
shuffling files
rescheduling meetings
avoiding phone calls
rushing through lunch
and daydreaming all afternoon.

Then I speed all the way home
quickly consume dinner
calmly undress
eagerly fall
into your arms
into love
and into a peaceful sleep.

Then once day breaks … I start all over.

You

Cause me to rise each morning with a smile
Give me extreme joy and make life worthwhile
Sing to my soul, embracing the man within.
Flow like a river, whose waters never end
Quench my thirst when the well runs dry
Are as lovely as a rainbow stretching across a sun lit sky
Accept my imperfections and nurture my dreams
Lift me up on your back when I have broken wings
Never hesitate to question me when you think I'm wrong
Always remain constant and your loyalty's strong

When I am disappointed, you console me
When I am lonely, you hold me

Your love shields me from the rain,
allowing only a few drops to dampen my head
So that when the sunshine reappears
I would appreciate the passing clouds

You are my reason for being, and it feels so damn good

Damon E. Johnson

Sunday Morning

She says she loves
the way my body feels
against hers
when we be making love
on Sunday mornings
like two sinners
on the way to Heaven
prior to getting dressed and
ready for service

Musing

The flowers don't smell as sweet
the sun doesn't shine quite the same
just like a game of hide and seek
with only a whisper of your name

The minutes, hours, and days go by
like they don't even exist
I struggle to find the reason why
the truth is, it's you that I miss

Damon E. Johnson

Now That's Jazz

The warmth
of your embrace
as passion takes its toll
The rhythm
of your heartbeat
as we lie soul to soul
The sweet sound
of your cries
when I'm loving you
The excitement
in your eyes, when
morning comes into view

Riesling

Confession

When was the last time someone told you
just how beautiful you are?
am I wrong to want to hold you
or even admire you from afar?

My feelings are not due to lack
or motivated by greed
I pray my motives don't come under attack
for admitting that it's you I need

There's just something about your smile
that mere words can not define
I've desired you for quite awhile
oh how I wish that you were mine

Desire

A few minutes of lust
poisoned by thoughts
of ever after
often leads to tears
conveniently lost in sweat.
Still our lips were not wise.

Damon E. Johnson

Who Am I to Fight It

The sun falls
into the night
The moon falls
into the morning
The rain falls
in the spring
The leaves fall
in autumn
Even empires
have been known to fall
So it's no secret that I'm falling for you
and who am I to fight it

Pillow Talk

Tell me that you love me
as we hold each other close
tell me I'm your one true desire
and that I'm the one you crave the most

Tell me all of your secrets
including your sexual fantasy
it doesn't really matter what it is
as long as you are sharing it with me

Tell me how you need to be loved
and how to speak to your heart
we have a lifetime ahead of us
but right now is a good place to start

Soul Mates

We were no more than strangers at best
yet our conversation seemed to just flow
now I think of you for days without rest
as our mutual interest starts to grow

Maybe this is just a start of a magical season
where angels appear right out of the blue
I'm certain our encounter has a purpose or reason
even though right now I don't have a clue

In my heart there's a raging passion
emotions are running high and can't be tamed
my mind wants me to be old fashion
but desire is calling your name

We never even touched, yet we are connected
like the same shadow cast by the sun
a feeling that refuse to be ignored or neglected
indeed the mating of our souls has just begun

Broken Butterfly

One day
when you least expect it
I'm going to capture you
with both of my hands
Surround you
with my cocoon of love
And then hold you
until you are again
beautiful

Damon E. Johnson

On Familiar Terms

You know what I'm thinking
before I say it
I can read your expression
before you display it

You know I do
when I say I don't
I know you will
when you say you won't

You feel my pain
when I'm hurt inside
I see right through you
when you try to hide

You are sometimes right
when I'm occasionally wrong
I am the music
you are the song

All or Nothing

Last night
I had a dream we were
making love on a tightrope
And it was one of the worlds
greatest romances
Our performance
inspired quite a bit of hope
But left no room for
second chances

7:45 Service

Your face is glowing
with quiet laughter
as I kiss you
between your thighs
Baptizing you with my tongue
just before anointing you, with oil

Life is Beautiful

Somewhere
There's a robin singing amongst the tall trees
There's a sun slowly dropping into the ocean
There's a child smiling for the first time
There's a couple sharing the same soul
There's a rainbow bending over the clouds
There's a butterfly riding the wind
There's a life being lived without caution
And if you blink, you just may miss your blessing

Damon E. Johnson

Chocolate Thighs

Dark and lovely
shade of brown
Soft and sexy
where I go down

Thick and curvy
along the hips
Sweet and tender
on my lips

I can see the future
in your eyes
As I lay waist deep
inside your thighs

Epiphany

Nightfall lured me into a wonderful dream
one that I will soon never forget
she made my pulse race and my body scream
and was gone before the sun and my eyes met

Morning found me in a state of confusion
how could she just up and disappear?
our encounter seemed like much more than an illusion
because the evidence of love was unquestionably clear

The warmth of her touch felt so real
yet somehow difficult to explain
though my excitement is hard to conceal
still quite a few questions remain

Did she descend from heaven, where the royal trumpets
can be heard? Was she an angel in disguise?
is beautiful the only suitable word that can describe
the color of her eyes?

Am I the only man she visits in the wee hours of the night,
or merely part of an elaborate scheme?
Could I be just a love starved dreamer, and she…
the essence my dream?

I Came

I walked
I strolled
I ran
I flew
      To your open arms.
I danced
I romanced
I laid
I stayed
      Long after the loving was over.
I came
To bring you joy.

Look of Love

If spoken words become complicated
and hallmark cards ever lose their feel
when text messages become outdated
and flowers no longer have appeal

If holding hands becomes old fashioned
and occasional phone calls become obsolete
when songs of love begin to lack passion
and small acts of kindness fall incomplete

If handwritten notes appear too sappy
and public affection becomes taboo
you will forever make my eyes happy
so baby… here's looking at you

Forbidden

Like eyes refusing light
Ears rejecting the truth
Lips determine not to touch
Arms resisting fulfillment
We must deny our purpose

Kaleidoscopic Sex

Dynamic and visual reflections
of extremely colorful imagery
symmetrically mirrored in
optical patterns of light
twisted and formed in
parallel illusions and
painted shadows
of complex
beauty

Damon E. Johnson

One Saturday Night in Autumn

We both became victims of an unexpected kiss
that seemed somewhat untimely for our season.
Patience was no longer a virtue worth exploring,
as the heat of the night penetrated our bare skin
and warmed our willing and hungering souls.
The fear of losing religion crossed our minds
while the guiltless spirituality that we were seeking
was unattainable without our bodies touching.
Thus, when Sunday morning finally arrived, we
looked forward to the sunrise and not a sermon.

Why

Why do I miss u since u been gone?
Why do I wish you were here?
Why every time I pick up the phone
It's your sweet voice I long to hear?

Why did the loving have to be so good to me?
Why do I still yearn for those soft lips?
Why couldn't I be the man that I should be?
Why did I let you slip through my fingertips?

And still I wonder…

Damon E. Johnson

Fulfilled Loneliness

Your embrace pulls me
deeper inside your treasure
as the sweat from our bodies
fall onto the sheets like rain
Your smile signifies your pleasure
as your mind fast forwards to the pain...
of me leaving you

Close Encounter

Meet me in a dream
so I can see your lovely face
meet me on the moon
where I can love you in space

Meet me on a rainbow
so I can slide down holding you
meet me on the sun
where any hot spot will do

Song of Slumber

Thoughts of you
consume my pen
as I quietly sit
alone at my desk
trying to recall
the words to the song
that often comes to my lips
in my dreams
when the day ends
and visions of you begin

A Good Woman

Got me a good woman
who loves making love
from scratch
Makes me wanna explode
every time she strikes
my match

Damon E. Johnson

The Gift

An unexpected act of
thoughtfulness
such a wonderful surprise

A sudden rush of
anticipation
that quickly turns to sighs

As you stand exposed
in front of me
unwrapped before my eyes

Summer Love

Like passion hard to keep
our souls run deep
Like the stars in the sky
your kisses take me high
Like tulips born in June
our love continues to bloom
Like no one else before
it's you that I adore

Damon E. Johnson

Love

Some people run from love because
they're too afraid to face it
Some people lose out on love because
they fail to embrace it
Some people think that love is a game
that you play to win
Some people spend more time falling out of love
than they do falling in
Some people constantly look for love
through rose colored glasses
Some people try to find love by
spreading themselves among the masses
Some people get tricked into love because
they're too eager to take the bait
Some people pray for love but
don't have the faith or patience to wait

If it's real you will know it
If you feel it you should show it
If you cherish it you won't blow it
If it is damaged you should restore it
If it's good you should enjoy it
If it's meant to be you can't ignore it
If it's a mystery you should explore it
If it's tied to a prayer you should wait for it
If its heaven sent you should adore it

The End of Words

When birds spurn flight
When moths avoid light
When flowers refuse rain
When hearts welcome pain
When soil rejects seeding
When lips deny needing
When fish abandon streams
When poets ignore dreams

Damon E. Johnson

Epilogue

Damon E. Johnson

About the Author

Damon E. Johnson is a freelance writer and poet currently residing in Atlanta, Georgia. The Vineyard: Exploding Grapes is his second book of poetry following his stellar debut collection, Rhythm in My Blues. Like fine wine this exploration of love and desire teases the palate as you experience the bitter and the sweet in an explosion of emotion released by his pen.

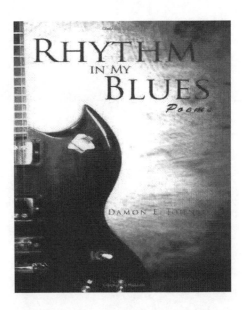

Damon E. Johnson's First Book

Made in the USA
San Bernardino, CA
30 May 2015

Damon's Links

Web

www.rhythminmyblues.com

Twitter

@Damonej28

Author Page

www.ctupublishinggroup.com/damon-e.-johnson-.html

Creative Talents Unl

Creative Talents Unleashed is a publ
that offers an inspiring platform for b
seasoned writers to tap into and particip
offer daily writing prompts and chall
the writer's mind, a variety of writi
much more. We are honored to assist w
and grow in the journey of becomin
authors.

For More Information

www.ctupublishinggroup.com

Creativetalentsunleashed@aol.